First published in Great Britain by Hamlyn
This edition published in 1996 by Chancellor Press
an imprint of Reed Consumer Books Limited,
Michelin House, 81 Fulham Road, London SW3 6RB

ISBN 1 85153 004 5

A CIP catalogue record for this book
is available from the British Library

ACKNOWLEDGEMENTS

Designed and produced by: The Bridgewater Book Company
Series Editors: Veronica Sperling and Christine McFadden
Art Director: Peter Bridgewater
Designer: Terry Jeavons
Photography: Trevor Wood
Food preparation and styling: Jonathan Higgins
Cookery contributor: Christine France

Produced by Mandarin Offset
Printed and bound in Singapore

NOTES

❦ Standard level spoon measurements are used in all recipes.
❦ Both imperial and metric measurements have been given in all recipes. Use one set of measurements only and not a mixture of both.
❦ Eggs should be size 3 unless otherwise stated.
❦ Milk should be full fat unless otherwise stated.
❦ Fresh herbs should be used unless otherwise stated. If unavailable use dried herbs as an alternative but halve the quantites stated.
❦ Ovens should be preheated to the specified temperature - if using a fan assisted oven, follow manufacturer's instructions for adjusting the time and the temperature.
❦ All microwave information is based on a 650 watt oven. Follow manufacturer's instructions for an oven with a different wattage.

Contents

Introduction

THE origin of the flan can be traced back several centuries. These days they are served at many different occasions, from formal dinners to the most informal snack. The words tart and flan are interchangeable, but quiche strictly speaking refers only to the classic Quiche Lorraine, which is filled with a savoury egg custard, often with ham and cheese added.

Choice of Tins

The traditional French flan tin with a loose base is perhaps the easiest choice for most savoury flans. Deeper metal fluted or plain rings, placed on a baking sheet, are an alternative for making slightly deeper flans. Ovenproof porcelain fluted flan dishes are attractive to bring to the table but they tend not to cook the pastry quite so crisply as metal containers, and removing the first slice of flan can be tricky.

Making the Pastry Case

Roll out the pastry evenly on a lightly floured surface slightly larger than your chosen tin, allowing for the depth.

Lift the pastry over the rolling pin, then place over the tin. Ease the pastry into the flan tin, taking care not to stretch it.

If the tin is fluted, use the back of your finger to press the pastry into each flute.

Lightly press back the pastry over the edges and run the rolling pin over the top edge to cut off any excess. Prick the base of the pastry all over with a fork.

Baking Blind

The main purpose of this is to ensure that the base is cooked and the pastry remains crisp, even with a wet filling.

To bake blind, line the uncooked pastry shell with greaseproof or non-stick kitchen paper, then fill this with dried beans, rice or pasta to weigh it down. (Keep the beans in a jar to use again.) Place on a baking sheet and bake in a preheated oven at 200°C/400°F/gas mark 6 for 15 minutes.

Calculating Quantities

When a recipe calls for a measured amount of pastry, e.g. 175 g/6 oz shortcrust pastry, this refers to the amount of flour used in the recipe. However, bought ready-made pastry (such as puff pastry and filo pastry) is referred to by total weight.

Shortcrust Pastry

MAKES 200 G/7 OZ TO FILL A 20–30 CM/8–9 INCH TIN

200 g/7 oz plain flour
pinch of salt
100 g/3½ oz butter, diced
2 tbsp cold water

SIFT the flour and salt into a bowl. Rub the butter into the flour until the mixture resembles fine breadcrumbs.
❦ Gradually stir in enough cold water to form a dough.
❦ Turn onto a lightly floured surface and roll out as required.

VARIATIONS: For Cheese Shortcrust Pastry, stir in 50 g/2 oz grated strong Cheddar or Parmesan cheese and ¼ teaspoon dry mustard powder before adding the water.

For Wholemeal Shortcrust Pastry, use half wholemeal and half white flour. You may also need to add a little more water.

Other flavourings can be added e.g. fresh herbs, lemon or orange zest, ground nuts, sesame seeds.

All-in-One Shortcrust Pastry

MAKES 225 G/8 OZ TO FILL A 23–25 CM/9–10 INCH TIN

225 g/8 oz plain flour
pinch of salt
150 g/5 oz soft (tub) margarine
1–2 tbsp cold water

PLACE one-third of the flour in a bowl with the salt, margarine and water. Mix well with a fork. Stir in the remaining flour to form a dough.
❦ Turn onto a lightly floured surface and roll out as required.

VARIATION: For All-in-One Cheese Shortcrust Pastry, stir in grated cheese and mustard powder as for Cheese Shortcrust Pastry, above.

Rich Shortcrust Pastry

MAKES 225 G/8 OZ TO FILL A 23–25 CM/9–10 INCH TIN

225 g/8 oz plain flour
1 tbsp icing sugar
175 g/6 oz butter or margarine, diced
1 egg yolk
2 tbsp water

SIFT the flour and sugar together. Make a well in the centre and add the butter and egg yolk. Blend together with the fingertips, adding the water to form a dough.
❦ Chill thoroughly before rolling out on a floured surface.

Tortilla Quiche

SERVES 4–6

1 quantity Cheese Shortcrust Pastry
2 tbsp vegetable oil
2 potatoes, diced
2 onions, diced
1 red pepper, seeded and diced
2 eggs, lightly beaten
300 ml/½ pint single cream
100 g/4 oz Cheddar cheese, grated
salt and freshly ground black pepper

ROLL out the pastry, and line a 23 cm/9 inch flan tin. Bake blind in a preheated oven at 200°C/400°F/gas mark 6 for 15 minutes.

❦ Heat the oil, and gently fry the potatoes and onions for 5–6 minutes. Add the red pepper, and cook until tender. Spoon the vegetables into the pastry case.

❦ Mix together the eggs, cream and cheese, and season to taste. Spoon the mixture over the vegetables.

❦ Bake at 190°C/375°F/gas mark 5 for 30–35 minutes until set. Serve hot or cold.

Quiche Provençale

SERVES 4–6

1 quantity Shortcrust Pastry
2 tbsp olive oil
1 onion, sliced
200 g/7 oz aubergine, sliced
200 g/7 oz courgettes, sliced
2 garlic cloves, crushed
1 red pepper, seeded and sliced
¼ tsp dried marjoram
¼ tsp dried thyme
1 tsp finely chopped fresh parsley
salt and freshly ground black pepper
2 eggs, lightly beaten
125 ml/4 fl oz single cream
75 g/3 oz Parmesan cheese, grated

ROLL out the pastry, and line a 23 cm/9 inch flan tin. Bake blind in a preheated oven at 200°C/400°F/gas mark 6 for 15 minutes.

❦ Heat the oil, and fry the onion until soft. Add the aubergine, courgettes, garlic and red pepper, and fry lightly. Stir in the herbs, and salt and pepper to taste. Continue cooking over a low heat until the vegetables are soft.

❦ Beat together the eggs, cream and Parmesan cheese. Remove the vegetables from the pan with a slotted spoon, and fold into the egg mixture. Pour carefully into the pastry case.

❦ Bake at 200°C/400°F/gas mark 6 for 30 minutes until set. Serve immediately.

Cheese and Watercress Flan

SERVES 4

- 1 quantity Shortcrust Pastry
- 175 g/6 oz cream cheese
- 4 tbsp soured cream
- 2 eggs, separated
- salt and freshly ground black pepper
- 2 tbsp chicken stock or water
- 2 tsp powdered gelatine
- 1 bunch watercress, about 50 g/2 oz, trimmed and finely chopped
- 4 spring onions, finely chopped
- 3 tbsp soured cream, to garnish
- coarsely chopped watercress, to garnish

ROLL out the pastry, and line a deep-sided, loose bottomed 20 cm/8 inch flan tin. Bake blind in a preheated oven at 200°C/400°F/gas mark 6 for 15 minutes.

❦ Beat together the cheese, soured cream, egg yolks and seasoning. Place the chicken stock and gelatine in a heatproof bowl, and set over a pan of hot water. Stir until the gelatine has dissolved, then beat into the cheese mixture. Set aside until on the point of setting.

❦ Whisk the egg whites until stiff. Fold into the cheese mixture, together with the watercress and spring onions. Spoon into the pastry case, and smooth the surface. Chill until set.

❦ Garnish by spreading the soured cream over the surface and sprinkling with the chopped watercress. Serve cold.

Ricotta and Red Onion Tart

SERVES 6

- 1 quantity All-in-One Cheese Shortcrust Pastry, made with Parmesan cheese
- 2 tbsp olive oil
- 450 g/1 lb red onions, thinly sliced
- 2 tbsp chopped fresh basil
- 1 egg, beaten
- 1 egg yolk
- 225 g/8 oz ricotta cheese
- 150 g/5 oz fromage frais
- salt and freshly ground black pepper
- 3 tbsp freshly grated Parmesan cheese

ROLL out the pastry, and line a 25.5 cm/10 inch flan tin. Bake blind in a preheated oven at 200°C/400°F/gas mark 6 for 15 minutes.

❦ Heat the oil in a large pan and fry the onions gently for about 10 minutes, until softened but not browned. Spread the onions over the base of the pastry case and scatter the basil on top.

❦ Beat together the eggs, ricotta cheese, fromage frais and salt and pepper, and pour into the pastry case.

❦ Sprinkle with the Parmesan cheese and bake at 190°C/375°F/gas mark 5 for 25–30 minutes until set.

Aubergine, Tomato and Mozzarella Flan

SERVES 4–6

1 quantity Shortcrust Pastry
5 tbsp olive oil
1 large aubergine, sliced
salt and freshly ground black pepper
4 tomatoes, peeled and sliced
175 g/6 oz mozzarella cheese, thinly sliced
2 tbsp chopped fresh basil
¼ tsp grated nutmeg
1 egg, beaten
150 ml/¼ pint passata (sieved tomatoes)
fresh basil, to garnish

ROLL out the pastry, and line a 23 cm/9 inch fluted flan tin. Bake blind in a preheated oven at 200°C/400°F/gas mark 6 for 15 minutes.

❦ Raise the oven temperature to 230°C/450°F/gas mark 8. Brush a baking sheet with some of the oil, and arrange the aubergine slices on the sheet in a single layer. Brush the slices with the remaining oil and sprinkle with salt and pepper. Bake for 25–30 minutes, turning once, until golden brown and soft.

❦ Arrange overlapping slices of the aubergine, tomato and mozzarella cheese in the pastry case, and sprinkle with the basil and nutmeg. Beat together the egg and passata then pour onto the filling.

❦ Reduce the oven temperature to 190°C/375°F/gas mark 5 and bake the flan for 45 minutes until golden brown and set. Garnish with fresh basil and serve hot.

Danish Quiche

SERVES 4

1 quantity Shortcrust Pastry
50 g/2 oz Danish Blue cheese, crumbled
100 g/4 oz Edam cheese, diced
25 g/1 oz butter, softened
2 eggs, lightly beaten
450 ml/16 fl oz milk
pinch of cayenne pepper
freshly ground black pepper
2 tbsp chopped spring onion

ROLL out the pastry, and line a 20 cm/8 inch flan tin. Bake blind in a preheated oven at 200°C/400°F/gas mark 6 for 15 minutes.

❦ Blend together the cheeses and butter with a fork. Add the eggs, and mix in the milk, seasoning and spring onion.

❦ Pour the mixture into the pastry case. Bake in a preheated oven at 190°C/375°F/gas mark 5 for 20–25 minutes until golden brown and set. Serve hot or cold.

Rich Broccoli and Cream Cheese Flan

SERVES 4

1 quantity Wholemeal Shortcrust Pastry
200 g/7 oz broccoli florets
150 g/5 oz cream cheese with garlic and herbs
4 eggs
150 ml/¼ pint milk
salt and freshly ground black pepper
4 spring onions, finely chopped

ROLL out the pastry, and line a 20.5 cm/8 inch fluted flan ring on a baking sheet. Bake blind in a preheated oven at 200°C/400°F/gas mark 6 for 15 minutes.

❦ Blanch the broccoli in boiling water for 3–5 minutes. Drain well and arrange in the pastry case.

❦ Beat together the cheese, eggs and milk. Season well with salt and pepper and add the onions. Pour into the pastry case.

❦ Bake at 190°C/375°F/gas mark 5 for 35–40 minutes, until set and golden brown. Serve hot or cold.

Dolcelatte and Almond Tart

SERVES 4–6

250 g/9 oz ready-made puff pastry
1 egg, beaten
3 tbsp ground almonds
150 g/5 oz dolcelatte cheese, diced
freshly ground black pepper
3 tbsp single cream
3 tbsp flaked almonds

ROLL out the pastry to a 25.5 cm/10 inch square and trim the edges with a sharp knife.

❦ Lift carefully onto a lightly oiled baking sheet. With a sharp knife, make two L-shaped cuts in the pastry, in opposite corners, about 2.5 cm/1 inch from the outer edges. Stop just short of joining the cuts into a square.

❦ Moisten the edges of the pastry with beaten egg. Lift one cut corner and draw it to the opposite side. Lift the other cut corner across to the opposite side, forming a square with raised edges.

❦ Prick the base of the pastry square with a fork, then sprinkle with the ground almonds.

❦ Arrange the diced cheese on top, keeping it away from the pastry edges, sprinkle with pepper then drizzle the cream over. Scatter with the flaked almonds. Glaze the pastry edges with beaten egg.

❦ Bake in a preheated oven at 220°C/425°F/gas mark 7 for 15–20 minutes until well-risen and golden brown. Serve hot.

Cheddar Soufflé Quiche

SERVES 4–6

1 quantity Cheese Shortcrust Pastry
50 g/2 oz butter
50 g/2 oz flour
300 ml/½ pint milk
2 eggs, separated
100 g/4 oz Cheddar cheese, finely grated
salt and freshly ground black pepper
1 egg white

Roll out the pastry, and line a 23 cm/9 inch flan tin. Bake blind in a preheated oven at 200°C/400°F/gas mark 6 for 15 minutes.

❦ Melt the butter, stir in the flour and cook, stirring constantly, for 2 minutes. Gradually stir in the milk. Cook, stirring until thick and smooth. Remove from the heat.

❦ Beat the egg yolks, cheese and seasoning into the sauce.

❦ Whisk all the egg whites until stiff, fold into the sauce and spoon into the pastry case. Bake at 190°C/375°F/gas mark 5 for 25–30 minutes until set. Serve immediately.

Courgette and Hazelnut Tart

SERVES 4

50 g/2 oz fresh wholemeal breadcrumbs
50 g/2 oz wholemeal flour
50 g/2 oz ground hazelnuts
2 tbsp melted butter
2 tbsp sunflower oil
1–2 tbsp water
1 small onion, finely chopped
25 g/1 oz butter or margarine
25 g/1 oz plain flour
150 ml/¼ pint stock
2 medium courgettes, coarsely grated
1 tbsp chopped fresh thyme
salt and freshly ground black pepper
25 g/1 oz hazelnuts, sliced

Mix together the breadcrumbs, wholemeal flour, ground hazelnuts, melted butter and oil. Stir in just enough water to bind together then press firmly into a 19 cm/7½ inch flan tin.

❦ Bake in a preheated oven at 200°C/400°F/gas mark 6 for 15 minutes, until crisp and golden.

❦ Fry the onion in the butter or margarine until softened. Stir in the flour and cook, stirring, for 1 minute.

❦ Add the stock and stir until thickened, then add the courgettes and cook for 2–3 minutes.

❦ Stir in the thyme and salt and pepper, then spoon into the pastry case. Sprinkle with the sliced nuts and bake for 10–15 minutes or until golden and bubbling. Serve hot or cold.

Tarte Pissaladière

SERVES 4

1 quantity Shortcrust Pastry
1 tbsp vegetable oil
1 large onion, chopped
1 garlic clove, crushed
400 g/14 oz can chopped tomatoes
1 bay leaf, crushed
¼ tsp dried thyme
¼ tsp dried oregano
salt and freshly ground black pepper
2 eggs, lightly beaten
100 g/4 oz gruyère or Emmenthal cheese, grated
50 g/2 oz can anchovies, drained, to garnish
6 pitted black olives, to garnish

ROLL out the pastry, and line a 22 cm/8½ inch flan tin. Bake blind in a preheated oven at 200°C/400°F/gas mark 6 for 15 minutes.

❦ Heat the oil, and gently fry the onion until soft. Add the garlic, tomatoes, herbs and salt and pepper to taste. Cook over a low heat for 20–30 minutes, stirring occasionally.

❦ Remove from the heat, and stir in the eggs and cheese. Pour into the pastry case, and carefully arrange the anchovies and olives on top.

❦ Bake in a preheated oven at 190°C/375°F/gas mark 5 for 25–30 minutes, until golden brown. Serve hot.

Walnut Tart

SERVES 4

1 quantity Wholemeal Shortcrust Pastry
40 g/1½ oz butter
1 large onion, sliced
1 red pepper, seeded and chopped
2 eggs, lightly beaten
150 ml/¼ pint milk
1 tsp yeast extract
freshly ground black pepper
100 g/4 oz walnuts, chopped
4–8 walnut halves, to garnish

ROLL out the pastry, and line a 22 cm/8½ inch flan tin. Bake blind in a preheated oven at 200°C/400°F/gas mark 6 for 15 minutes.

❦ Melt the butter, and gently fry the onion and pepper for 3-5 minutes. Beat together the eggs, milk and yeast extract, and season to taste.

❦ Place the onion and pepper in the pastry case, and sprinkle with the chopped walnuts. Pour on the egg and milk mixture.

❦ Bake in a preheated oven at 190°C/375°F/gas mark 5 for about 30 minutes until set.

❦ Garnish the tart with the walnut halves and serve hot or cold.

Little Chèvre Tartlets

SERVES 4–8

200 g/7 oz filo pastry
4 tbsp walnut or hazelnut oil
15 g/½ oz butter
4 spring onions, finely chopped
150 g/5 oz soft goat cheese
2 eggs, beaten
150 ml/¼ pint milk (or goat milk)
salt and freshly ground black pepper
1 tbsp wholegrain mustard
4 tbsp wholemeal breadcrumbs
paprika, to garnish

BRUSH each sheet of filo pastry with the oil and cut into twenty four 12.5 cm/5 inch squares. Arrange overlapping slices in 8 individual flan tins, about 10 cm/4 inches diameter.

❦ Melt the butter and fry the onions over a low heat for about 1 minute. Remove from the heat and stir in the cheese.

❦ Beat together the eggs, milk, salt, pepper and mustard, then stir in the onions and cheese. Pour into the pastry cases and sprinkle with the breadcrumbs.

❦ Bake in a preheated oven at 190°C/375°F/gas mark 5 for 15–20 minutes until the filling is set and the pastry golden brown. Serve hot, sprinkled with paprika.

Red and Yellow Pepper Tart

SERVES 4–6

1 quantity Shortcrust Pastry
1 large red pepper, seeded and sliced
1 large yellow pepper, seeded and sliced
1 small onion, thinly sliced
2 garlic cloves, crushed
2 tbsp olive oil
4 tbsp dry white wine or stock
2 eggs
2 egg yolks
150 ml/¼ pint single cream
salt and freshly ground black pepper
10 pitted black olives

ROLL out the pastry, and line a 23 cm/9 in fluted flan tin. Bake blind in a preheated oven at 200°C/400°F/gas mark 6 for 15 minutes.

❦ Meanwhile, gently fry the peppers, onion and garlic in the olive oil for 3–4 minutes, stirring. Add the wine or stock and cook over a low heat until the vegetables are softened.

❦ Beat the eggs and egg yolks together, then add the cream and salt and pepper. Spread the pepper mixture in the pastry case with the olives and pour in the egg mixture.

❦ Bake at 190°C/375°F/gas mark 5 for 30–35 minutes until golden brown and set. Serve hot or cold.

Onion and Olive Tart

SERVES 4

1 quantity Shortcrust Pastry
25 g/1 oz butter
700 g/1½ lb onions, sliced
225 ml/8 fl oz chicken stock
freshly ground black pepper
2 tbsp double cream
1 green pepper, seeded and sliced
10 pitted black olives
75 g/3 oz gruyère cheese, grated
2 tbsp olive oil

ROLL out the pastry, and line a 22 cm/8½ inch flan tin. Bake blind in a preheated oven at 200°C/400°F/gas mark 6 for 15 minutes.

❦ Melt the butter, and gently fry the onions until translucent. Stir in the stock and season to taste. Cook, stirring constantly, until all the liquid has evaporated. Remove the pan from the heat and stir in the cream.

❦ Spoon the onion mixture into the pastry case. Arrange the green pepper and olives on top. Sprinkle with the cheese and olive oil.

❦ Bake at 190°C/375°F/gas mark 5 for 25–30 minutes. Serve immediately.

Mushroom Cream Quiche

SERVES 4–6

1 quantity Shortcrust Pastry
25 g/1 oz butter
1 small onion, chopped
225 g/8 oz small button mushrooms
150 ml/¼ pint plain yogurt
150 ml/¼ pint double cream
3 eggs, lightly beaten
2 tsp dried mixed herbs
2 tsp snipped fresh chives or chopped spring onion tops
salt and freshly ground black pepper

ROLL out the pastry, and line a 23 cm/9 inch flan tin. Bake blind in a preheated oven at 200°C/400°F/gas mark 6 for 15 minutes.

❦ Melt the butter, and gently fry the onion for 5 minutes until softened. Add the mushrooms, and cook for 2–3 minutes. Remove the pan from the heat.

❦ Mix together the yogurt, cream and eggs. Add to the mushroom mixture, blending well. Stir in the dried herbs and chives or spring onions and season to taste.

❦ Spoon the mixture into the pastry case, and bake at 190°C/375°F/gas mark 5 for 30–35 minutes until golden brown and set. Serve hot or cold.

Spicy Tofu and Bean Flan

SERVES 4–6

200 g/7 oz plain flour
100 g/3½ oz butter or margarine
100 g/4 oz frozen chopped spinach, thawed and well drained
1 tbsp sunflower oil
1 small onion, chopped
1 large red pepper, seeded and diced
½ tsp chilli powder
200 g/7 oz can red kidney beans, drained and rinsed
275 g/10 oz packet silken tofu
1 tsp light soy sauce
salt and freshly ground black pepper
2 tbsp sesame seeds

SIFT the flour and rub in the butter or margarine evenly. Stir in the spinach and mix to a fairly soft dough.

❦ Roll out the pastry, and line a 23 cm/9 inch fluted flan tin. Prick the base and bake blind in a preheated oven at 200°C/400°F/gas mark 6 for 15 minutes.

❦ Heat the oil and fry the onion and pepper for 4–5 minutes to soften. Stir in the chilli powder and kidney beans.

❦ Purée the tofu in a food processor then stir in the soy sauce and seasoning. Stir the tofu into the vegetables and spoon into the pastry case. Sprinkle with the sesame seeds and bake at 190°C/375°F/gas mark 5 for 20–25 minutes. Serve hot or cold.

Fennel and Camembert Tart

SERVES 4–6

1 quantity Rich Shortcrust Pastry
1 tbsp olive oil
1 small fennel bulb, finely chopped
150 g/5 oz camembert cheese, diced
2 tbsp chopped fresh parsley
2 tomatoes, peeled and diced
1 egg, beaten
1 egg yolk
150 ml/¼ pint crème fraîche
salt and freshly ground black pepper

ROLL out the pastry, and line a 23 cm/9 inch fluted flan tin. Bake blind in a preheated oven at 200°C/400°F/gas mark 6 for 15 minutes.

❦ Heat the oil and fry the fennel until soft. Spoon into the pastry case with the cheese, parsley and tomatoes.

❦ Beat together the egg and egg yolk, crème fraîche and seasonings, then pour onto the filling.

❦ Bake at 180°C/350°F/gas mark 4 for 25–30 minutes until set and golden brown. Serve hot or cold.

VARIATION: For Celery and Brie Tart, use 175 g/6 oz celery, thinly sliced, instead of the fennel, and substitute brie for the camembert cheese. Bake and serve as in the main recipe.

Cheese and O ion Rice Tart

SERVES 6

1 quantity Rich Shortcrust Pastry
25 g/1 oz butter
1 small leek, thinly sliced
1 garlic clove, crushed
225 g/8 oz short-grain rice
1 tsp turmeric
600 ml/1 pint chicken stock
3 spring onions, chopped
finely grated zest of 1 lemon
2 tbsp chopped fresh parsley
salt and freshly ground black pepper
1 egg, beaten
75 g/3 oz cream cheese
50 g/2 oz mozzarella cheese, grated or chopped
50 g/2 oz freshly grated Parmesan cheese

ROLL out the pastry, and line a 25.5 cm/10 inch fluted flan tin. Bake blind in a preheated oven at 200°C/400°F/gas mark 6 for 15 minutes.

❦ Melt the butter and gently fry the leek until soft. Stir in the garlic, rice, turmeric and stock. Cover and simmer gently until the rice is tender and the liquid absorbed.

❦ Add the onions, lemon zest, parsley and seasonings. Beat together the egg and cream cheese and stir into the rice.

❦ Spread the rice mixture into the pastry case and sprinkle the mozzarella and Parmesan cheeses in lines over the top.

❦ Bake at 190°C/375°F/gas mark 5 for 25–30 minutes, or until golden brown and bubbling. Serve hot or cold.

Tomato Tart

SERVES 4

1 quantity Shortcrust Pastry
700 g/1½ lb tomatoes
15 g/½ oz butter
1 large onion, sliced
½ small fresh red chilli, sliced
1 garlic clove, crushed
salt and freshly ground black pepper
onion rings, to garnish

ROLL out the pastry, and line a 22 cm/8½ inch flan tin. Bake blind in a preheated oven at 200°C/400°F/gas mark 6 for 15 minutes.

❦ Peel and roughly chop 450 g/1 lb of the tomatoes. Melt the butter, and fry the onion, chilli and garlic for 1 minute. Add the chopped tomatoes and season to taste. Cover and simmer for about 30 minutes until the tomatoes have formed a purée.

❦ Pour the purée into the pastry case. Thinly slice the remaining tomatoes, and arrange them over the tart, together with the onion rings. Bake at 190°C/375°F/gas mark 5 for 25–30 minutes. Serve hot or cold.

Golden Carrot Tart

SERVES 4–6

1 quantity Shortcrust or Cheese Shortcrust Pastry
450 g/1 lb carrots, sliced
2 tbsp orange juice
3 tbsp sunflower seeds
3 eggs, separated
50 g/2 oz Double Gloucester cheese, grated
salt and freshly ground black pepper

ROLL out the pastry and line a 23 cm/9 inch flan tin. Bake blind in a preheated oven at 200°C/400°F/gas mark 6 for 15 minutes.

❦ Cook the carrots in boiling water for 8–10 minutes until tender. Drain well and purée in a food processor with the orange juice and half the sunflower seeds.

❦ Beat in the egg yolks and cheese. Season well.

❦ Whisk the egg whites until stiff and fold into the carrot mixture. Spoon into the pastry case and sprinkle with the remaining sunflower seeds.

❦ Bake for 25–30 minutes until risen and golden brown. Serve immediately.

Mediterranean Pesto and Pine Nut Tartlets

SERVES 6

1 quantity Rich Shortcrust Pastry
2 eggs, beaten
200 ml/7 fl oz milk
2 tbsp pesto
4 tbsp freshly grated Parmesan cheese
salt and freshly ground black pepper
75 g/3 oz sun-dried tomatoes, chopped
50 g/2 oz pine nuts, toasted
50 g/2 oz gruyère cheese, grated

ROLL out the pastry, and line six 10 cm/4 inch fluted flan tins. Bake blind in a preheated oven at 200°C/400°F/gas mark 6 for 10 minutes.

❦ Beat together the eggs, milk, pesto, Parmesan cheese, and salt and pepper. Sprinkle the sun-dried tomatoes and half the pine nuts into the pastry cases and pour in the egg mixture. Bake at 190°C/375°F/gas mark 5 for 10 minutes.

❦ Mix the gruyère cheese with the remaining pine nuts and sprinkle on top of the tartlets. Bake for a further 10 minutes or until golden brown then serve hot.

Spinach and Cheese Quiche

SERVES 6–8

1 quantity Cheese Shortcrust Pastry
350 g/12 oz cottage cheese, sieved
1 egg, lightly beaten
3 egg yolks, lightly beaten
150 ml/¼ pint soured cream
½ tsp freshly grated nutmeg
salt and freshly ground black pepper
800 g/1½ lb frozen spinach, thawed and drained thoroughly
50 g/2 oz Cheddar cheese, grated
¼ tsp cayenne pepper

ROLL out the pastry, and line a 28 cm/11 inch flan tin. Bake blind in a preheated oven at 200°C/400°F/gas mark 6 for 15 minutes.

❦ Mix together the cottage cheese, egg, egg yolks and soured cream. Stir in half the nutmeg and season to taste.

❦ Arrange the spinach on the bottom of the pastry case, season and sprinkle over the remaining nutmeg. Pour in the cottage cheese mixture.

❦ Mix together the grated Cheddar cheese and cayenne pepper, and sprinkle evenly on top of the filling.

❦ Bake at 190°C/375°F/gas mark 5 for 35–40 minutes until golden brown and set. Serve hot.

Oyster Mushroom, Coriander and Parmesan Tart

SERVES 4–6

350 g/12 oz ready-made puff pastry
25 g/1 oz butter
2 shallots, finely chopped
100 g/4 oz oyster mushrooms, sliced
3 tbsp chopped fresh coriander
3 eggs, beaten
150 ml/¼ pint double cream
salt and freshly ground black pepper
4 tbsp freshly grated Parmesan cheese

ROLL out the pastry, and line a 23 cm/9 inch fluted flan tin. Bake blind in a preheated oven at 220°C/425°F/gas mark 7 for 5 minutes.

❦ Melt the butter and gently fry the shallots for 3–4 minutes to soften, then stir in the mushrooms and cook for a further 2–3 minutes, until soft. Spoon into the pastry case. Sprinkle with the coriander.

❦ Beat together the eggs, cream, and salt and pepper, and pour into the pastry case. Sprinkle with the Parmesan cheese.

❦ Bake at 180°C/350°F/gas mark 4 for 20–25 minutes, until golden brown and set. Serve hot.

West Country Flan

SERVES 4–6

- 1 quantity Shortcrust Pastry
- 8 rashers smoked lean streaky bacon, chopped
- 50 g/2 oz butter or margarine
- 700 g/1½ lb leeks, sliced
- 25 g/1 oz plain flour
- 300 ml/½ pint dry cider
- 100 g/4 oz mature Cheddar cheese, grated
- 3 tbsp double cream
- salt and freshly ground black pepper

Roll out the pastry, and line a deep 23 cm/9 inch flan tin. Bake blind in a preheated oven at 200°C/400°F/gas mark 6 for 15 minutes.

❦ Fry the bacon without fat until lightly browned. Stir in half the butter, add the leeks and continue to cook, stirring, until the leeks are soft.

❦ Melt the remaining butter in a saucepan and stir in the flour. Cook, stirring, for 1 minute, then gradually stir in the cider. Cook, stirring, until thickened and smooth.

❦ Remove from the heat and stir in the cheese, cream and seasonings. Add to the bacon and leeks, then spoon into the pastry case.

❦ Bake at 190°C/375°F/gas mark 5 for 30-35 minutes, until golden brown. Serve hot.

Salami and Tomato Flan

SERVES 4–6

- 1 quantity Wholemeal Shortcrust Pastry with 1 tbsp poppy seeds added
- 3 tbsp wholemeal breadcrumbs
- 1 tbsp chopped fresh rosemary
- 175 g/6 oz salami, thinly sliced and cut into strips
- 2 medium tomatoes, sliced into wedges
- 2 eggs, beaten
- 150 ml/¼ pint milk
- ½ tsp chilli sauce
- ¼ tsp garlic salt

Roll out the pastry, and line a 23 cm/9 inch fluted flan tin. Bake blind in a preheated oven at 200°C/400°F/gas mark 6 for 15 minutes.

❦ Sprinkle the breadcrumbs and rosemary over the base of the pastry case. Arrange the salami and tomatoes on top.

❦ Beat together the eggs, milk, chilli sauce and garlic salt. Pour into the pastry case. Bake at 190°C/375°F/gas mark 5 for 30–35 minutes, or until set and golden. Serve hot or cold.

Jellied Chicken and Herb Flan

SERVES 4–6

1 quantity Rich Shortcrust Pastry
3 rashers streaky bacon, diced
50 g/2 oz button mushrooms, sliced
1 chicken stock cube
2 tsp powdered gelatine
150 ml/¼ pint dry white wine
225 g/8 oz cooked chicken, diced
2 tbsp chopped fresh mixed herbs

ROLL out the pastry, and line a 23 cm/9 inch plain flan tin. Cut the trimmings into long thin strips and twist 2 together. Moisten the pastry rim with water and press the twist around the edge to decorate.

❦ Bake blind in a preheated oven at 200°C/400°F/gas mark 6 for 15 minutes. Remove the baking beans and bake for a further 5–10 minutes, until the pastry is cooked. Cool.

❦ Fry the bacon without fat until lightly browned, stir in the mushrooms and cook until soft. Cool. Dissolve the stock cube in 150 ml/¼ pint boiling water and stir in the gelatine until dissolved. Add the wine and allow to cool but not to set.

❦ Fill the pastry case with the chicken, bacon, mushrooms, herbs and seasoning. Pour in the gelatine mixture when it is on the point of setting. Chill for at least 1 hour until set. Serve cold.

VARIATION: For Chicken and Celery Barquettes, replace the mushrooms with diced celery. Roll out the pastry thinly, and line 20–24 individual barquette (boat-shaped) tins, or small fluted tartlet tins. Prick the bases and bake blind as above. Cool, fill and chill until set.

Curried Chicken Tartlets

SERVES 4

1 quantity Shortcrust Pastry
2 tsp curry powder
2 tbsp lemon juice
350 g/12 oz cold cooked chicken, skinned and cut into thin strips
100 g/4 oz walnuts, roughly chopped
125–150 ml/4–5 fl oz mayonnaise
salt and freshly ground black pepper
2 tbsp finely chopped fresh parsley

DIVIDE the pastry into 4 pieces. Roll out each piece, and line four 11.5 cm/4½ inch tartlet tins. Bake blind in a preheated oven at 200°C/400°F/gas mark 6 for 15 minutes.

❦ Stir the curry powder, lemon juice, chicken and walnuts into the mayonnaise, and season to taste. Spoon into the cold pastry cases, and smooth the surface. Sprinkle with the chopped parsley. Serve cold.

Spanish Pork and Orange Tart

SERVES 4–6

1 quantity Shortcrust Pastry
1 tbsp olive oil
1 small onion, thinly sliced
225 g/8 oz lean shoulder pork, cut into small dice
3 rashers smoked bacon, chopped
1 garlic clove, crushed
1 orange
2 tbsp fresh chopped parsley
25 g/1 oz pitted black olives, chopped
1 egg, beaten
150 ml/¼ pint soured cream
25 g/1 oz fresh breadcrumbs
orange segments, to garnish

ROLL out the pastry, and line a 23 cm/9 inch fluted flan tin. Bake blind in a preheated oven at 200°C/400°F/gas mark 6 for 15 minutes.

❦ Heat the oil and fry the onion, pork and bacon until lightly coloured. Add the garlic and remove from the heat. Grate the rind from the orange. Add to the meat with the parsley and olives. Beat together the egg, soured cream and seasoning. Cut away the peel and pith from the orange, and divide the flesh into segments.

❦ Sprinkle the breadcrumbs into the pastry case. Spoon in the meat mixture and orange segments. Spread with the soured cream. Bake at 180°C/350°F/gas mark 4 for 25–30 minutes, until golden. Serve hot, garnished with orange segments.

Chicken and Pepper Tart

SERVES 4–6

1 quantity Shortcrust Pastry
15 g/½ oz butter
1 onion, sliced
1 garlic clove, crushed
450 g/1 lb cold cooked chicken, skinned and diced
1 red pepper, seeded and sliced
1 green pepper, seeded and sliced
1 tbsp tomato purée
1 egg, lightly beaten
125 ml/4 fl oz double cream
½ tsp dried thyme
1 tbsp finely chopped fresh parsley
salt and freshly ground black pepper

ROLL out the pastry, and line a 23 cm/9 inch flan tin. Bake blind in a preheated oven at 200°C/400°F/gas mark 6 for 15 minutes.

❦ Melt the butter and lightly fry the onion and garlic. Add the chicken and cook until it begins to colour. Stir in the peppers, fry briefly then stir in the tomato purée.

❦ Beat together the egg, cream, herbs and seasoning to taste. Stir in the chicken mixture, then spoon into the pastry case.

❦ Bake at 190°C/375°F/gas mark 5 for 30–35 minutes until set.

Quickie Storecupboard Quiche

SERVES 4

- 275 g/10 oz packet frozen shortcrust pastry, thawed
- 275 g/10 oz can condensed chicken or chicken and mushroom soup
- 4 eggs, beaten
- 50 g/2 oz Cheddar cheese, grated
- parsley sprigs, to garnish

ROLL out the pastry, and line a 20.5 cm/8 inch fluted flan tin. Bake blind in a preheated oven at 200°C/400°C/gas mark 6 for 15 minutes. With small cutters, cut small star or heart shapes from the pastry trimmings.

❦ Beat together the soup and eggs, pour into the pastry case and sprinkle with the cheese. Arrange the pastry shapes on top and bake for 30–35 minutes until golden brown and set. Serve hot or cold, garnished with parsley.

Turkey and Cranberry Lattice Tart

SERVES 4

- 1 quantity All-in-One Shortcrust Pastry
- 75 g/3 oz sage and onion dry stuffing mix
- 225 ml/8 fl oz boiling water
- 175 g/6 oz cooked turkey, diced
- 75 g/3 oz fresh or frozen cranberries
- 2 tbsp cranberry jelly
- 2 tbsp orange juice
- salt and freshly ground black pepper

ROLL out three-quarters of the pastry, and line a 18 cm/7 inch square flan tin.

❦ Make up the stuffing mix with the boiling water according to the packet instructions. Spoon the stuffing into the pastry case and level the surface.

❦ Mix the turkey and cranberries with the cranberry jelly, orange juice, and salt and pepper. Spread over the stuffing mixture and press down evenly.

❦ Roll out the remaining pastry, cut into thin strips, and arrange in a lattice over the tart.

❦ Bake in a preheated oven at 190°C/375°F/gas mark 5 for 30–40 minutes, or until the pastry is firm and golden brown. Serve hot or cold.

Quiche Paysanne

SERVES 4–6

1 quantity Wholemeal Shortcrust Pastry
2 tbsp olive oil
25 g/1 oz butter
1 onion, sliced
4 rashers back bacon, chopped
50 g/2 oz button mushrooms, quartered
225 g/8 oz cooked potato, diced
salt and freshly ground black pepper
2 eggs, beaten
150 ml/¼ pint single cream or milk
50 g/2 oz Cheddar cheese, grated

ROLL out the pastry, and line a 23 cm/9 inch fluted flan tin. Bake blind in a preheated oven at 200°C/400°F/gas mark 6 for 15 minutes.

❦ Heat half the oil and butter in a large pan and fry the onion and bacon for 3–4 minutes, until golden. Stir in the mushrooms and cook until softened. Remove and place in the pastry case.

❦ Add the remaining oil and butter to the pan and stir in the potatoes. Cook, stirring occasionally, for about 10 minutes or until golden.

❦ Add the potatoes to the pastry case and season well with salt and pepper.

❦ Beat together the eggs and cream or milk and pour into the pastry case. Sprinkle with the grated cheese.

❦ Bake for 20–25 minutes or until golden and set. Serve hot.

Ham and Smoked Cheese Flan

SERVES 4

1 quantity Wholemeal Shortcrust Pastry
175 g/6 oz cooked ham, chopped
100 g/4 oz smoked cheese, finely diced
3 eggs, lightly beaten
150 ml/¼ pint single cream
¼ tsp freshly grated nutmeg
salt
3 tomatoes, sliced
sprigs of dill, to garnish

ROLL out the pastry, and line a 20 cm/8 inch flan tin. Bake blind in a preheated oven at 200°C/400°F/gas mark 6 for 15 minutes.

❦ Sprinkle the ham and cheese over the base of the pastry case. Mix together the eggs, cream, nutmeg and salt to taste, and spoon on top of the ham and cheese.

❦ Bake at 190°C/375°F/gas mark 5 for 25–30 minutes until set. Serve hot or cold, topped with the tomato slices and garnished with dill sprigs.

Beef and Potato Clock Flan

SERVES 4–6

100 g/4 oz plain flour
3 oz/75 g butter or margarine
100 g/4 oz mashed potato
1 tbsp sunflower oil
1 onion, chopped
225 g/8 oz lean minced beef
1 tsp dried mixed herbs
1 tbsp Worcestershire sauce
227 g/8 oz can chopped tomatoes
1 tbsp tomato purée

SIFT the flour and rub in the fat. Stir in the potato, season, and knead to a dough. Chill for 15 minutes.

❦ Roll out the pastry on a floured surface, and line a 23 cm/ 9 inch flan dish, reserving the trimmings.

❦ Heat the oil and fry the onion for 3–4 minutes. Add the beef and fry until lightly coloured. Add the herbs, Worcestershire sauce, tomatoes and tomato purée, and bring to the boil. Simmer for 3–4 minutes then spoon into the flan case.

❦ Roll out the pastry trimmings, and using cutters or a sharp knife cut out the numbers and hands of a clock. Arrange over the flan to resemble a clock face.

❦ Bake in a preheated oven at 180°C/350°F/gas mark 4 for 40–45 minutes. Serve hot.

Sausage Pizza Slice

SERVES 4

225 g/8 oz self-raising flour
50 g/2 oz butter or block margarine
7 tbsp milk
1 tbsp olive oil
1 onion, thinly sliced
1 tbsp plain flour
225 g/8 oz can chopped tomatoes
2 tbsp tomato purée
1 garlic clove, crushed
1 tsp dried oregano
125 ml/4 fl oz milk
4 cooked pork sausages, sliced
100 g/4 oz mozzarella cheese, diced
4 stuffed green olives, sliced

SIFT the flour with a pinch of salt into a mixing bowl, and rub in the butter evenly. Stir in the milk and mix to a soft dough. Roll out the pastry, and line a 22 x 30.5 cm/ 8½ x 12 inch rectangular shallow tin. Crimp the pastry edges.

❦ Heat the oil and fry the onion for 2–3 minutes to soften. Stir in the flour and cook for 2 minutes. Add the tomatoes, tomato purée, garlic, oregano and milk. Season and simmer until thickened. Spread the filling over the pastry and scatter the sausages, cheese and olives on top.

❦ Bake in a preheated oven at 200°C/400°F/gas mark 6 for 30–35 minutes until golden. Serve cut into fingers or squares.

Chicken, Cauliflower and Walnut Flan

SERVES 4–6

1 quantity Shortcrust Pastry
½ cauliflower, divided into florets
1 tbsp vegetable oil
2 boneless, skinless chicken breasts, cut into 2 cm/¾ inch pieces
1 onion, finely chopped
3 eggs, lightly beaten
150 ml/¼ pint single cream
75 g/3 oz walnuts, chopped
2 tbsp snipped fresh chives
pinch of grated nutmeg
salt and freshly ground black pepper
50 g/2 oz Cheddar cheese, grated

ROLL out the pastry, and line a 23 cm/9 inch flan tin. Bake blind in a preheated oven at 200°C/400°F/gas mark 6 for 15 minutes.

❦ Blanch the cauliflower florets in boiling water for 3 minutes. Drain, and arrange over the base of the pastry case.

❦ Heat the oil, and stir-fry the chicken pieces for 5 minutes. Remove from the pan. Add the onion to the pan, and fry for 5 minutes.

❦ Mix together the eggs, cream, walnuts, chives and nutmeg and season to taste. Stir in the chicken and cheese, then add to the onion. Mix well, and pour into the pastry case.

❦ Bake at 190°C/375°F/gas mark 5 for 40 minutes or until the filling is firm and golden brown. Serve hot or cold.

Sausagemeat and Apple Slice

SERVES 4

1 quantity Shortcrust Pastry with 2 tsp mixed dried herbs added
250 g/9 oz pork sausagemeat
3 tbsp fresh breadcrumbs
1 small onion, finely chopped
1 celery stick, thinly sliced
2 Cox's or other crisp eating apples
salt and freshly ground black pepper
25 g/1 oz Cheddar or Edam cheese, grated

ROLL out the pastry, and line a 34 x 10 cm/13½ x 4 inch rectangular flan tin. Bake blind in a preheated oven at 200°C/400°F/gas mark 6 for 15 minutes.

❦ Mix together the sausagemeat, breadcrumbs, onion and celery. Peel, core and finely chop 1 of the apples and stir into the sausagemeat mix. Season with salt and pepper.

❦ Spread the sausagemeat mixture evenly over the pastry case. Core and thinly slice the remaining apple and arrange over the flan. Sprinkle with the cheese and bake at 180°C/350°F/gas mark 4 for 40–45 minutes, until golden brown. Serve hot or cold, cut into slices.

Ham and Mixed Vegetable Quiche

SERVES 4

1 quantity Cheese Shortcrust Pastry
25 g/1 oz butter
1 small red pepper, seeded and sliced
1 small green pepper, seeded and sliced
50 g/ 2 oz mushrooms, thinly sliced
1 small courgette, very thinly sliced
75 g/3 oz cooked ham, chopped
2 eggs, lightly beaten
150 ml/¼ pint double cream
1 tbsp freshly grated Parmesan cheese
salt and freshly ground black pepper

ROLL out the pastry, and line a 20 cm/8 inch flan tin. Bake blind in a preheated oven at 200°C/400°F/gas mark 6 for 15 minutes.

❦ Melt the butter, and gently fry the peppers, mushrooms and courgette for 5 minutes. Sprinkle the ham over the base of the pastry case, then top with the pepper mixture.

❦ Beat together the eggs, cream, Parmesan cheese and seasoning to taste. Pour into the pastry case.

❦ Bake at 190°C/375°F/gas mark 5 for 30–35 minutes until set. Serve hot or cold.

Bacon, Tomato and Cheese Flan

SERVES 4–6

1 quantity Cheese Shortcrust Pastry
25 g/1 oz butter
1 garlic clove, crushed
2 onions, sliced
450 g/1 lb tomatoes, peeled
1 tbsp tomato purée
1 tsp dried mixed herbs
1 tsp sugar
50 g/2 oz smoked cheese, grated
4 streaky bacon rashers, rinded and cut in half lengthways
13 black olives, pitted and halved

ROLL out the pastry, and line a 23 cm/9 inch flan tin. Bake blind in a preheated oven at 200°C/400°F/gas mark 6 for 15 minutes.

❦ Melt the butter, and fry the garlic and onions for 8–10 minutes. Chop half the tomatoes, and add to the pan. Stir in the tomato purée, herbs, sugar and pepper to taste, and simmer for 5 minutes. Remove from the heat and cool slightly.

❦ Spoon the tomato and onion mixture into the pastry case. Slice the remaining tomatoes, and arrange on top. Sprinkle with the cheese, and arrange the bacon in a lattice on top. Place an olive half in each of the gaps.

❦ Bake at 190°C/375°F/gas mark 5 for 30–35 minutes until the cheese is golden. Serve hot.

Bacon and Sweetcorn Quiche

SERVES 4–6

1 quantity Shortcrust Pastry
15 g/½ oz margarine
6 streaky bacon rashers, rinded and chopped
1 small onion, finely chopped
200 g/7 oz can sweetcorn, drained
2 eggs, lightly beaten
200 ml/7 fl oz milk
1 tsp dried thyme
salt and freshly ground black pepper

ROLL out the pastry, and line a 23 cm/9 inch loose-bottomed flan tin. Bake blind in a preheated oven at 200°C/400°F/gas mark 6 for 15 minutes.

❦ Melt the margarine, and fry the bacon and onion until the onion is soft. Drain and transfer to the pastry case. Cover with the sweetcorn.

❦ Lightly beat together the eggs and milk, add the thyme and season to taste. Pour into the pastry case.

❦ Bake at 190°C/375°F/gas mark 5 for 30–35 minutes until golden brown and set. Serve hot or cold.

Chicken Liver and Sage Tartlets

SERVES 4–8

8 slices white or wholemeal bread
75 g/3 oz butter
1 shallot, finely sliced
225 g/8 oz chicken livers, chopped
100 g/4 oz open mushrooms, sliced
1 garlic clove, crushed
1 tbsp chopped fresh sage
3 tbsp dry sherry or red wine
125 ml/4 fl oz crème fraîche or single cream
salt and freshly ground black pepper
sage leaves, to garnish

CUT the crusts from the bread and trim to 8 cm/3½ inch squares. Press into 8 deep patty tins.

❦ Melt 50 g/2 oz of the butter and brush over the bread. Bake in a preheated oven at 200°C/400°F/gas mark 6 for 10–12 minutes, until golden brown and crisp.

❦ Meanwhile, melt the remaining butter and fry the shallot for 1–2 minutes, to soften.

❦ Add the chicken livers and fry until lightly coloured, then stir in the mushrooms and garlic. Cook, stirring, for 2 minutes then add the sage and sherry or wine.

❦ Simmer for 1 minute, then stir in the crème fraîche or cream, and cook for a further 2 minutes to reduce slightly.

❦ Season with salt and pepper and spoon into the bread cases. Serve hot, garnished with sage leaves.

Quiche Lorraine

SERVES 4

1 quantity Shortcrust or Cheese Shortcrust Pastry
15 g/½ oz butter
1 tbsp finely chopped onion
2 streaky bacon rashers, rinded and chopped
225 ml/8 fl oz single cream
50 g/2 oz Cheddar cheese, grated
1 egg, lightly beaten
salt and freshly ground black pepper
pinch of paprika

ROLL out the pastry, and line a 20 cm/8 inch flan tin. Bake blind in a preheated oven at 200°C/400°F/gas mark 6 for 15 minutes.

❦ Melt the butter, and fry the onion and bacon until they begin to colour. Add the cream, and heat until a rim of bubbles forms, but do not allow to boil.

❦ Remove the pan from the heat, add the cheese and stir until it has melted. Stir in the egg, and season to taste with salt, pepper and paprika.

❦ Pour the mixture into the pastry case, and bake at 190°C/375°F/gas mark 5 for 25–30 minutes, until golden brown and set. Serve hot or cold.

Spiced Lamb Tart with Apricots

SERVES 4

10 sheets filo pastry
5 tbsp olive oil
1 medium onion, finely chopped
225 g/8 oz lean minced lamb
1 tsp ground cumin
1 tsp ground coriander
2 tsp chopped fresh ginger root
100 g/4 oz no-soak dried apricots, chopped
1 egg, beaten
75 ml/3 fl oz Greek-style yogurt
salt and freshly ground black pepper

BRUSH each sheet of pastry with olive oil and arrange in layers, overlapping at different angles, in a 20.5 cm/8 inch flan tin. Scrunch up the pastry around the edges.

❦ Heat 1 tablespoon of the oil in a large pan and fry the onion until soft. Stir in the lamb and fry until lightly coloured.

❦ Stir in the cumin, coriander, ginger and apricots. Cover and simmer gently for 10 minutes. Remove from the heat.

❦ Beat together the egg and yogurt, season well with salt and pepper then stir into the meat mixture. Spoon the mixture into the pastry case, and bake in a preheated oven at 190°C/375°F/gas mark 5 for 20–25 minutes, until the pastry is golden and the filling set. Serve hot.

Creamy Scallop and Emmenthal Tart

SERVES 4–6

1 quantity Rich Shortcrust Pastry
2 shallots, finely chopped
25 g/1 oz butter
8 large scallops, with corals
1 tbsp chopped fresh parsley
1 tbsp chopped fresh coriander
salt and freshly ground black pepper
75 g/3 oz Emmenthal cheese, grated
2 eggs, beaten
150 ml/¼ pint single cream

ROLL out the pastry, and line a 23 cm/9 inch fluted flan tin. Bake blind in a preheated oven at 200°C/400°F/gas mark 6 for 15 minutes.

❦ Fry the shallots in the butter until softened but not browned. Carefully remove the orange corals from the scallops and slice the white flesh.

❦ Stir the white flesh and corals into the shallots with the parsley, coriander, and salt and pepper. Remove from the heat.

❦ Spoon the scallop mixture into the pastry case, and sprinkle with the cheese. Beat together the eggs and cream then pour into the pastry case.

❦ Bake at 180°C/350°F/gas mark 4 for 25–30 minutes or until set. Serve hot.

Smoked Salmon and Minted Cucumber Cream Flans

SERVES 4

1 quantity Shortcrust Pastry
175 g/6 oz cucumber, peeled and finely chopped
100 g/4 oz cream cheese
4 tbsp mayonnaise
2 tbsp chopped fresh mint
75 g/3 oz smoked salmon trimmings, chopped
salt and freshly ground black pepper
cucumber slices and mint sprigs, to garnish

ROLL out the pastry, and line 12 deep patty tins or small fluted flan tins. Prick the bases and bake in a preheated oven at 200°C/400°F/ gas mark 6 for 15 minutes or until the pastry is golden brown and crisp. Cool.

❦ Meanwhile, place the cucumber in a colander and leave to drain for 30 minutes.

❦ Beat together the cream cheese and mayonnaise until smooth, then stir in the mint, cucumber and salmon. Season to taste.

❦ Spoon the filling into the cooled pastry cases and smooth over. Garnish with cucumber and mint and serve cold.

Tuna, Sweetcorn and Iceberg Quiche

SERVES 4

1 quantity Wholemeal Shortcrust Pastry
¼ iceberg lettuce, shredded
200 g/7 oz can tuna in oil, drained and flaked
200 g/7 oz can sweetcorn, drained
2 tbsp snipped fresh chives
2 eggs, beaten
150 ml/¼ pint single cream
salt and freshly ground black pepper

ROLL out the pastry, and line a 20.5 cm/8 inch square fluted flan tin. Bake blind in a preheated oven at 200°C/400°F/gas mark 6 for 15 minutes.

❦ Arrange the lettuce, tuna and sweetcorn in the pastry case and sprinkle with the chives.

❦ Beat together the eggs and cream, season well with salt and pepper and pour into the flan case.

❦ Bake at 190°C/375°F/gas mark 5 for 20–25 minutes until set and lightly browned. Serve hot or cold.

Smoked Haddock and Tomato Flan

SERVES 4

1 quantity Wholemeal Cheese Shortcrust Pastry
225 g/8 oz smoked haddock or cod
200 ml/7 fl oz milk
1 bay leaf
225 g/8 oz cherry tomatoes, halved
25 g/1 oz butter
25 g/1 oz plain flour
2 eggs, beaten
3 tbsp double cream
salt and freshly ground black pepper
chopped fresh parsley, to garnish

ROLL out the pastry, and line a 20.5 cm/8 inch fluted flan ring on a baking sheet. Bake blind in a preheated oven at 200°C/400°F/gas mark 6 for 15 minutes.

❦ Place the fish in a pan with the milk and bay leaf. Bring to the boil, cover and cook over a low heat for about 10 minutes or until the fish flakes easily.

❦ Drain and reserve the milk. Flake the fish and arrange in the pastry case with the tomatoes.

❦ Melt the butter in a pan and stir in the flour. Cook, stirring, for 1 minute, then gradually stir in the milk. Stir over a moderate heat until thickened and smooth.

❦ Cool slightly then beat in the eggs, cream, and salt and pepper to taste.

❦ Pour the sauce into the pastry case and bake for a further 25–30 minutes or until golden brown and set. Serve hot, sprinkled with parsley.

Salmon Quiche

SERVES 4–6

1 quantity Shortcrust Pastry
25 g/1 oz butter
1 large onion, finely chopped
2 tbsp chopped green pepper
200g/7 oz can salmon, drained and flaked
pinch of cayenne pepper
salt and freshly ground black pepper
150 ml/¼ pint single cream
3 eggs, lightly beaten
50 g/2 oz Cheddar cheese, grated
50 g/2 oz pitted green olives, chopped

ROLL out the pastry, and line a 23 cm/9 inch flan tin. Bake blind in a preheated oven at 200°C/400°F/gas mark 6 for 15 minutes.

❦ Melt the butter, and fry the onion for 5 minutes. Stir in the green pepper, salmon and cayenne pepper, and season to taste. Cook for 2 minutes, then allow to cool.

❦ Mix together the cream, eggs, cheese and olives. Stir into the salmon and pepper mixture, and pour into the pastry case.

❦ Bake at 200°/400°F/gas mark 6 for 40 minutes until golden brown and firm. Serve hot or cold.

Avocado Seafood Tarts

SERVES 4

150 g/5 oz filo pastry
25 g/1 oz butter, melted
6 crab sticks, chopped
100 g/4 oz peeled cooked prawns
1 avocado
1 tbsp lemon juice
1 tsp cornflour
1 tbsp milk
100 g/4 oz Greek-style yogurt
1 tbsp chopped fresh thyme
1 garlic clove, crushed
salt and freshly ground black pepper
sprigs of parsley, to garnish

CUT the pastry sheets into twelve 10 cm/4 inch squares. Brush with the melted butter, and line 4 individual fluted brioche tins, in 3 overlapping layers. Bake in a preheated oven at 200°C/400°F/gas mark 6 for 5 minutes.

❦ Mix together the crab sticks and prawns. Halve the avocado, remove the stone, scoop out the flesh and dice. Toss in the lemon juice and stir into the fish. Spoon into the pastry cases.

❦ Blend the cornflour with the milk and stir into the yogurt. Stir in the thyme, garlic, and salt and pepper then pour onto the filling.

❦ Bake at 190°C/375°F/gas mark 5 for 15–20 minutes. Serve hot, garnished with parsley sprigs.

Creamy Kipper Brunch Flan

SERVES 4–6

1 quantity Shortcrust or Cheese Shortcrust Pastry
100 g/4 oz long-grain rice
salt and freshly ground black pepper
350 g/12 oz cooked kipper fillets, sliced
2 hard-boiled eggs
125 ml/4 fl oz single cream
1 tsp mild curry paste
1 tbsp chopped fresh parsley
chopped fresh parsley and lemon slices, to garnish

ROLL out the pastry, and line a 23 cm/9 inch fluted flan tin. Bake blind in a preheated oven at 200°C/400°F/gas mark 6 for 15 minutes. Remove the beans and bake for a further 15 minutes or until crisp and golden.
❦ Cook the rice in boiling, lightly salted water for 12–15 minutes or until tender. Drain well and mix with the kippers.
❦ Chop the eggs and stir into the rice mixture with the cream, curry paste, parsley, and salt and pepper.
❦ Spoon into the pastry case and spread evenly. Garnish with parsley and lemon slices and serve hot.

Sardine Cartwheel Flan

SERVES 4

6 thin slices granary bread, crusts removed
40 g/1½ oz butter or margarine, melted
1 egg, beaten
75 g/3 oz fromage frais
salt and freshly ground black pepper
2 medium tomatoes, sliced
100 g/4 oz can sardines in oil, drained and halved lengthways

CUT the bread slices in half diagonally to make triangles. Brush a 20.5 cm/8 inch flan dish with some of the melted butter, and line with overlapping bread slices, pressing down firmly. Brush with the remaining butter.
❦ Bake blind in a preheated oven at 200°C/400°F/gas mark 6 for 10 minutes, then remove the beans and paper and bake for a further 10 minutes.
❦ Beat together the egg, fromage frais and salt and pepper, and spoon into the bread case. Arrange the tomato slices and sardines on top, in a wheel shape.
❦ Bake for a further 15–20 minutes, or until golden brown. Serve hot.

Cheesy Cod and Parsley Slice

SERVES 4

1 quantity Shortcrust Pastry with 1 tbsp finely grated lemon zest added
225 g/8 oz cod fillet, skinned and diced
100 g/4 oz mature Cheddar cheese, grated
2 tbsp chopped fresh parsley
200 ml/7 fl oz milk
2 eggs, beaten
salt and freshly ground black pepper

ROLL out the pastry, and line a 19 cm/7½ inch square plain flan tin or sandwich cake tin. Roll out the trimmings and cut out small fish shapes with a cutter or knife.

❦ Arrange the cod in the pastry case, and sprinkle with the cheese and parsley.

❦ Beat together the milk, eggs, and salt and pepper, and pour into the pastry case.

❦ Moisten the pastry edges and place the fish shapes around the top edge, pressing lightly. Brush with milk to glaze.

❦ Bake in a preheated oven at 180°C/350°F/gas mark 4 for 35–40 minutes, or until golden brown. Serve hot.

Prawn Tartlets

SERVES 6

1 quantity Shortcrust Pastry
15 g/½ oz butter
1 onion, sliced
225 g/8 oz cooked peeled prawns
1 egg, lightly beaten
100 g/4 oz cream cheese
2 tbsp double cream
2 tsp finely chopped fresh parsley
salt and freshly ground black pepper
cooked whole prawns, to garnish
1 tsp finely chopped fresh parsley, to garnish

ROLL out the pastry, and line 6 individual tartlet tins. Bake blind in a preheated oven at 200°C/400°F/gas mark 6 for 5 minutes.

❦ Melt the butter, and gently fry the onion for about 3 minutes. Remove from the heat.

❦ Stir in the prawns, egg, cream cheese, cream and parsley. Season to taste. Spoon the filling into the tartlet cases.

❦ Bake at 190°C/375°F/gas mark 5 for 15–20 minutes until golden brown and set.

❦ When cold, garnish the tartlets with the whole prawns and parsley, and serve.

Smoked Mackerel and Horseradish Tart

SERVES 4–6

75 g/3 oz plain flour
150 g/5 oz rolled oats
150 g/5 oz sunflower margarine
1 small onion, thinly sliced
1 tbsp sunflower oil
225 g/8 oz smoked mackerel fillets, skinned and chopped
2 eggs, beaten
150 g/5 oz cottage cheese
1 tbsp creamed horseradish
1 tbsp chopped fresh dill
3 tbsp milk
salt and freshly ground black pepper
sprigs of dill, to garnish

Mix together the flour and oats and rub in the margarine evenly. Mix to a dough, adding a little cold water, if necessary.

❦ Roll out the pastry, and line a 34 x 10 cm/13½ x 4 inch rectangular flan tin. Prick the base and bake blind in a preheated oven at 200°C/400°F/gas mark 6 for 15 minutes.

❦ Fry the onion in the oil for 2–3 minutes to soften. Place in the pastry case with the mackerel.

❦ Beat together the eggs, cottage cheese, horseradish, dill, milk, and salt and pepper, then pour into the pastry case.

❦ Bake at 190°C/375°F/gas mark 5 for 25 minutes, or until set and golden. Serve hot or cold, garnished with dill.

Tuna and Mushroom Quiche

SERVES 4

1 quantity Shortcrust Pastry
15 g/½ oz butter
1 large onion, chopped
1 garlic clove, crushed
175 g/6 oz mushrooms, sliced
200 g/7 oz can tuna, drained
125 ml/4 fl oz milk
2 eggs, lightly beaten
2 tbsp double cream
1 tbsp finely chopped fresh parsley
salt and freshly ground black pepper

Roll out the pastry, and line a 22 cm/8½ inch flan tin. Bake blind in a preheated oven at 200°C/400°F/gas mark 6 for 15 minutes.

❦ Melt the butter, and gently fry the onion, garlic and mushrooms for 3–5 minutes.

❦ Flake the tuna and arrange the flaked fish over the base of the pastry case. Cover with the onion and mushroom mixture.

❦ Beat together the milk, eggs, cream and parsley, and season to taste. Pour the egg mixture into the pastry case.

❦ Bake at 190°C/375°F/gas mark 5 for about 30 minutes. Serve hot or cold.

Smoked Salmon Quiche

SERVES 6–8

1 quantity Cheese Shortcrust Pastry
225 g/8 oz cream cheese, softened
4 eggs, lightly beaten
4 egg yolks, lightly beaten
2 tbsp lemon juice
175 g/6 oz smoked salmon, cut into thin strips
300 ml/½ pint single cream
½ tsp cayenne pepper
sprigs of dill, to garnish

ROLL out the pastry, and line a 28 cm/11 inch flan tin. Chill in the refrigerator for 15 minutes.

❦ Place the cheese in a bowl and gradually beat in the eggs and egg yolks. Stir in the lemon juice, salmon and cream. Add the cayenne and some pepper. Pour into the pastry case.

❦ Bake in a preheated oven at 190°C/375°F/gas mark 5 for 30–35 minutes until golden brown and set. Serve cold.

Mussel Tartlets

SERVES 6–8

200 g/7 oz ready-made puff pastry
75 g/3 oz butter
2 shallots, chopped
1 garlic clove, crushed
1.5 litres/2¼ pints mussels, scrubbed and bearded
200 ml/7 fl oz water
7 tbsp dry white wine
2 tbsp finely chopped fresh parsley
salt and freshly ground black pepper
25 g/1 oz flour
2 egg yolks
200 ml/7 fl oz double cream
chopped fresh parsley, to garnish

ROLL out the pastry, and line 6–8 tartlet tins. Bake blind in a preheated oven at 220°C/425°F/gas mark 7 for 10–12 minutes. Remove the baking beans and lining, and return the tartlet cases to the oven for a further 3 minutes.

❦ Melt half the butter, and briskly fry the shallots and garlic for 1 minute. Add the mussels, water, wine and parsley, season to taste, cover and boil until the mussels open.

❦ Drain the mussels, discarding any that have not opened. Strain and reserve the cooking liquid.

❦ Melt the remaining butter, and stir in the flour. Cook, stirring constantly for 1 minute. Gradually stir in 300 ml/½ pint of the reserved cooking liquid. Simmer, stirring constantly, until thick and smooth. Stir in the egg yolks, but do not allow to boil. Remove from the heat, and season to taste.

❦ Remove the mussels from their shells. Divide equally between the tartlets, pour on the sauce, and heat through under a moderate grill. Garnish with parsley, and serve hot.